SEVEN REASONS

WHY EVERY LOCAL CHURCH SHOULD HAVE A MINISTRY TRAINING CENTER

Stan E. DeKoven

SEVEN REASONS

WHY EVERY LOCAL CHURCH
SHOULD HAVE A MINISTRY TRAINING CENTER

ISBN: 978-1-61529-003-1

2ND EDITION

PUBLISHED BY:

Vision Publishing
1115 D Street
Ramona, CA 92065
1-800-9-VISION
WWW.VISIONPUBLISHINGSERVICES.COM

ALL SCRIPTURE REFERENCES ARE TAKEN FROM THE
NEW INTERNATIONAL VERSION OF THE BIBLE,
UNLESS OTHERWISE NOTED.

FOREWARD

In Dr. Peter Wagner's seminal work on the New Apostolic Reformation, *"Church Quake"*[1] (pages 234-239), Dr. Wagner summarizes a most important trend in training men and women for ministry. A shift of monumental importance has occurred, moving theological education from the regional seminary to the local church, from the hallowed halls of academia to the streets where God's people live.

Dr. Wagner calls these new educational ministries "New Apostolic Schools," designed to create home grown staff through innovative and radical teaching paradigms. These programs de-emphasize the gaining of degrees as the primary goal (options) at the expense of dynamic skill building. Further, Dr. Wagner lists seven key elements of these schools, which provide significant insight as to why they are effectively preparing leaders in the 21st century.

1. The training center in a New Apostolic School (NAS) is flexible in the faculty they choose. Rather than academic credentials alone to determine

---

[1] Reference C Peter Wagner, *Churchquake,* Regal Books 1999

competence, calling of God and empowerment by the Spirit are even more important. By and large, the local pastor will determine who teaches with guidance by educational experts they are in relationship with. Thus...

2. Anointing counts as highly as degrees. However, most New Apostolic Schools will use men and women with a unique combination of both education and the ability to impart life. The instructors are challenged to teach head and heart in combination, using a very selective and flexible curriculum. This flexibility can be seen in...

3. A curriculum that is broad in perspective and centered on specific end results. The curriculum will generally include such standard courses as Old and New Testament, Hermeneutics, Homiletics and the like, but will also contain dynamic courses in practical ministry and such topics as Spiritual Warfare, Strategic Missions planning, and Deeper Life studies. Further, the New Apostolic Schools are...

4. Flexible in delivery system, which is designed more for the adult learner than the typical college student. The class schedule could be integrated within traditional Sunday School programs, Mid-Week services, 1-2 nights a week part time program, or even weekend seminars, combining dynamic instruction with distance learning. Further, with the emergence of the Internet, many NAS are developing or networking with others to develop continuing education opportunities for people in their stream of ministry or network influence. Of course, the place for this instruction is...

5. The local church or the church in the locality. The Bible College or Training Institute comes under apostolic oversight, which provides the key governmental leadership to the school. In some locals, the NAS is actually a regional school sponsored and supported by key city leaders, a breeding ground for advanced unity in action, a most exciting phenomenon. Many of these schools are linked relationally...

6. In a voluntary relationship with other degree granting schools. Most of these schools come under the umbrella of the Apostolic Council for Educational Accountability headquartered in Colorado Springs, CO. Finally, these schools are filled with...

7. The expectation that the graduates of their schools will be key leaders in the nations, filled with anticipation of great and wonderful things being done in the name of Jesus around the world.

The times are changing. The belief is that the world is reachable for Christ, more now than at any other time in history. We are asking the Lord of the Harvest for laborers, and New Apostolic Schools are putting feet to their prayers.

ACKNOWLEDGMENTS

I would like to thank the faculty and staff of Vision International University, and especially Dr. Randy Gurley, my partner in planting Bible Colleges around the world. I also want to acknowledge the Resource Center Directors of Vision International Education Network, who have encouraged me in all areas of my ministry, especially in my writing endeavors.

It is my hope that this book will be a blessing to our entire Network, students in other Bible Colleges and future Adult Education programs both nationally and internationally.

It is for you that this book has been written.

My special thanks go to Bishop Paul E. Paino, now with the Lord, for his encouragement in writing this book and making it available to participants in the World Missions.

I must also acknowledge my colleagues in the Apostolic Council for Educational Accountability. Thanks for providing the inspiration and motivation to write in validation of our divine call.

TABLE OF CONTENTS

INTRODUCTION

NETWORKS FOR TRAINING

There are wonderful changes taking place today in the Body of Christ. While many congregational and independent ministries are conducting business as usual, some are putting on new wine skins by establishing new ministry approaches, initiated by a season of unified, cooperative service in God's Kingdom for His greater purposes. This new paradigm, a return to New Testament Christianity, has been coined by Dr. C. Peter Wagner as the New Apostolic Reformation. A part of this new paradigm, or new wineskin, is the return of educational ministry to its proper and biblical roots: training in the local church.

Both in the world and in the church, the word "network" is being used to identify a revolutionary concept vital to fulfilling God's master plan. Networking, which is the willful and strategic working together in a win-win proposition, presents a glorious sign of divine life that will lead to the unprecedented revival we pray for and genuinely expect.

In 1990, God instructed us to start a network of Bible

Colleges.[2] Our mandate was to take "The Whole Word to the Whole World," bringing discipleship ministry to the nations. By faith we entered into covenant relationships with local church pastors possessing apostolic vision, whereby we (Vision) provide services to local congregations for the ministry training of God's people in a given community. This covenant relationship has proven to provide ongoing mutual blessing.

Recently, God has been challenging me to higher levels of leadership, along with greater revelation of His intentions for the 21st century.

I never intended to be a Bible College or Seminary instructor, let alone to start a non-traditional University with a worldwide network of church-based colleges. In fact, I was fairly content giving leadership to a large group counseling ministry, but God had other ideas!

In some ways, it was two "chance" encounters with two presidents of other Bible colleges which were in a network together that started me down this long eventful road. The most influential contact was with my dear friend Dr. Ken Chant. Dr Ken, an Australian by birth, was pastor of a problematic fellowship located across the freeway from my main counseling office. I had received a referral to counsel one of his flock, and called him out of professional courtesy and for good public relations. A few days later we met, thus beginning a wonderfully functional relationship.

---

[2] Vision International Education Network, Vision International University, originally as Vision Christian College, Australia.

Dr. Chant had crossed the waters of the Pacific to expand his teaching and writing ministry. He came to San Diego to establish his Vision Bible College program in what was then a large local church. The circumstances in that church deteriorated, but rising out of its ruins came Vision's present program, with the concept of taking this successful teaching ministry to the cities of the world. Under the direction of the Holy Spirit, we launched our network of schools, which now reaches over 140 nations, training thousands of leaders, bringing discipleship ministry to the nations for God's glory.

Our present and any future success will always be a result of calling and gifting, but primarily of God's grace. As the network has grown, so has our understanding of the theological and strategic importance of our work.

We are convinced, and would love to persuade every man and woman in leadership of the church, that every local church (for a more detailed understanding, see definitions in Appendix I) have a Bible/Ministry Training Center.

Of course, this is my burning passion, created in my heart through the vision given me by the Lord, echoed in Habakkuk 2:14, *"For the earth will be filled with the knowledge of the glory of the LORD, as the waters cover the sea."*

It is my hope that you will take a serious look with me at the key reasons every local church should have a dynamic, Spirit-led Bible college program for the training of God's people, moving them into their individual gifting and calling.

There are many wonderful institutions of higher education that train men and women for service: the best laboratory for training engineers, computer scientists, mathematicians, lawyers, etc., may well be a centralized university with ample resources. In like manner, the best laboratory for training Christian leaders for service within Jesus' Church is the local church in each city.

There are many excellent programs (See Appendix II) which will help establish such programs as ours, training leaders to fulfill the vision God has for them. We must follow the New Testament pattern of equipping people in local churches, and then releasing men and women of God into dynamic, life changing ministry.

CHAPTER ONE

PRINCIPLE 1: THE CRISIS

THE LACK OF LEADERS AND THE LOSS OF
SONS AND DAUGHTERS

Over the past fifteen years I have heard these two stories over and over again. The first is the lack of loyal leaders to work hand in hand with the pastor in the harvesting of souls. Pastors labor to win souls, preaching to them, counseling them in time of need, only to see them leave over some small offense, joining another congregation in the same city, starting the tragic cycle all over again.

Jesus told us to pray for laborers for His harvest, a prayer He intended to have answered through trained disciples (Matt 9:10). The lack of leaders within the local church can be traced to the lack of a strategic plan to train leaders, due to faulty models, lack of resources or a wrong paradigm of ministry. All too often, in our transient society, people have been taught to cut and run whenever hard times come, demonstrating a lack of faithfulness and loyalty that fills the heart of leaders with dismay. It is a terrible and unnecessary loss!

Another tragedy I see occurs when the pastor, generally a man of high integrity, with a deep love for his flock, endures the loss of a spiritual son or daughter of the local church to a regional college or university. These gifted men of God have a vision to train leaders, and desire only the very best for their people, God's heritage.

Often the young man or woman has been saved in the local church and has been faithfully discipled by the local pastoral staff. However, when they reach age eighteen, and especially if a call of God is upon their life, a decision must be made as to where and how they are to be trained for full-time ministry or Christian service. Until recently, the only options were to send them to a regional training center, Bible College, or Liberal Arts University for their education. This has been justified as the "best we can do" for our young person, since our primary model for education has been the centralized, government accredited programs that many pastors had to suffer with.

Since there have been few, if any alternatives, the conscientious local church pastor would honestly attempt to assist the young person to make an informed decision as to which would be the best institution to attend. Unfortunately, horror stories are only too often the result. The stories include the stark reality that the once tender and hungry student in the local church becomes unteachable at best, and all too often they never return to the local church from which they came.

The causes of this phenomenon are many. They

include the liberal agenda found in even the most conservative of regional colleges and universities. But this is only part of the problem. Add to this the agenda of the academic community at large, which has advocated the separation of the head from the heart, the Word from the Spirit. The focus of the regional school has only been the education of the mind, leaving little room for the training of the man and woman of God for the dynamics of a Spirit-filled ministry in a local assembly. Some notable quotes from a few expert resources might help to clarify just how problematic this situation truly is.

There have been four consequences to the scholastic, academic focus of seminaries:

1. The separation of Head from Heart.
2. The separation of Theological Education from Church Life and Ministry.
3. The Seminary has come to be viewed as a poor investment for ministry preparation.
4. Entrenched traditionalism has led to seminaries being structurally irreformable.

This started in North America at Harvard College in 1636. "Harvard College was created by the civil government and governed by a board of overseers, or trustees, made up equally of clergy and magistrates...[This followed the] Reformation model, which was one step more secular in the sense of being less directly under church control. The Reformers ... depended on the princes for their success. Seminary founders ... assumed that the day-by-day skills needed by the clergy would be learned in the give and take of [local church] community life.

Nineteenth-century seminaries were the houses that theology built." (As quoted in *The History of Seminary Education and Theological Accreditation,* by Dr. Gary Greig, presented at the Apostolic Council for Educational Accountability, Colorado Springs, CO, June, 1999).

The standard models of seminary training are painfully out of touch with the average Christian. George Barna, President of The Barna Institute reports (as presented in the provisional catalog of the Wagner Leadership Institute, 1998) that "most pastors agree that they were inadequately trained for the job of leading the local church. Yet, seminaries continue to forge ahead, providing much of the same irrelevant (and in some cases, misleading and harmful) education that has been their forte for the past century. One response has been churches creating their own ministry education centers to raise up leaders and teachers from within their congregations. Another response has been for churches to hire believers who have secular training and experience in professional fields and allow them to learn the content of ministry realities while they are on the job. There is little doubt that churches are in desperate need of effective leadership as the challenges confronting the church become more complex, more numerous and more daunting."

"But how will those leaders be identified, developed and nurtured for effective ministry leadership? Is there a role for the seminary in the future of the church? If so, what should that seminary look like and what would its ideal role be? If churches continue to rely on seminaries — or some alternative developmental structure — to provide them with leaders, it is imperative that the leader training grounds be reshaped. Mere tinkering with a broken system won't provide the answer; creating a holistic, strategic, and intelligently-crafted process is needed."

This indictment against the "White Elephant" of standard seminary education has resulted in many new and exciting adaptations.

The very model of education and training recommended by our culture is different from and hostile to the model found in the Word of God. The New Testament model for education, especially preparation for ministry, is the apostolic pattern of training church leaders described in the Book of Acts. The pattern, detailed in chapter 4, is found in Acts, chapters 2 (Jerusalem), 11- and 13 (Antioch), 14 (Lystra, Iconium, and Pisidian Antioch) and 19 (Ephesus). Each city where Peter or Paul ministered became a discipleship or training center. When the proper vision of the great commission was in the forefront of the apostles' teaching, the church grew and God was glorified. This model is the only one that will reduce or eliminate the twin crises of a lack of leadership, and the tragedy of losing sons and daughters to the world or the regional, state-approved, often-too-liberal College or University.

CHAPTER TWO

PRINICIPLE 2: THE CONCERN

THE PURPOSE OF TEACHNG IS
TO BE LIKE THE MASTER

THE WORD AND TEACHING

Teaching is the primary vehicle for the transmitting of cultural truth and biblical revelation from generation to generation.[3] Throughout God's dealings with His people, He has commanded them to know the commandments and to teach them, so that all might live the commandments out in their daily experience. This process is supposed to continue from generation to generation.

In Psalm 143:10 the Word of God says, *"Teach me to do your will."* One of the primary purposes of the teaching ministry is to help people to know what the will of God is and then to do it. This teaching, as stated in Deuteronomy 4:9, begins at the earliest age. It says, *"Teach them to your*

---

[3] This chapter is excerpted from the book, *Christian Education: Principles & Practice*, by Dr. Stan E. DeKoven.

children." Teaching and training is a process that begins in the family long before a child experiences a Sunday School Program, Children's Church, or attends a private Christian school. It is the responsibility of the parents to teach their children and to teach them well, with a primary purpose:

To Win the Hearts

Evangelism is to be a primary focus of teaching.

Psalm 51:13 states, *"I will teach transgressors your ways."*

Everyone involved in local church leadership should have the ability to teach. That does not mean that each one is a gifted teacher, but they must be capable of communicating the truth of God's Word with clarity and purpose. Titus 2:1 states, *"You must teach what is in accord with sound doctrine* (or sound teaching)." Paul admonishes his son in the Lord, Titus, to teach properly and systematically so that a clear understanding of God's purposes for His people is gained. The teaching process is not to be mere "rambling-on" about whatever someone feels. It is a specific process of imparting divine truth found within the Word of Clod, bringing structural and permanent change in the lives of students. Thus, our focus is always:

To Equip the Saints

A primary scripture that emphasizes the importance of teaching in the Christian church is Ephesians 4:11. Here, Paul the Apostle teaches that the five-fold ministry, apostles, prophets, evangelists, pastors, and teachers are all necessary components in the ministry of perfecting the saints or bringing them to Christian maturity. The entire five-fold ministry, as elders, must be able to teach, imparting relevant truth from God's precious Word.

Also, in I Corinthians 12:28 teaching is presented as one of the ministry gifts to the church. Thus, within the New Testament church, teaching was, and continues to be, a vital function to be exercised consistently. However, teaching is not teaching unless the student has demonstrated:

That They Have Learned

The purpose of teaching should be to ensure that learning actually occurs. Just because someone is talking at the front of a classroom does not mean that learning is actually taking place. Probably the greatest thrill a teacher can have is to see the light come on in a learner's mind. No real teaching has taken place unless truth has become relevant to the student, which makes it applicable in their life. That is why learning is incomplete until it has become a part of the student's repertoirc of knowledge and experience.

II Timothy 3:7, KJV says, *"Ever learning, and never able to come to the knowledge of the truth."* That is the tragedy that many people experience. They spend much time in reading, studying and learning (not experiential), but never practicing what has been learned in a life of effective service.

Church leaders are to be sufficiently prepared so as to

become effective transmitters of God's truth. This truth is to be applied by the student for active use in real life. In this regard, the Word of God speaks clearly and profoundly. A teacher is to:

> *"Study to show thyself approved unto God, a workman that needeth not to be ashamed, rightly dividing the word of truth."* (II Timothy 2:15, KJV)

> *"...because you know that we who teach will be judged more strictly."* (James 3:1)

> *"They want to be teachers of the law, but they do not know what they are talking about or what they so confidently affirm."* (I Timothy 1:7)

The teacher, functioning within a local church setting, with apostolic/pastoral authority, has an awesome and delightful responsibility! To equip God's people for His service in the kingdom is an honor indeed, and our labor is:

For His Reward

It would be a great tragedy if, after a life of teaching, we stood before the Lord to hear Him state that what we had taught His people was only wood, hay, and stubble rather than gold, silver, and precious stones.

> Hebrews 5:12 says, *"In fact, though by this time you ought to be teachers, you need someone to teach you the elementary truths of God's word all over again. You need milk, not solid food!"*

There are many ways to view this Bible passage. Some commentators have stated that the "students" spoken of must have been dull or ignorant. However, perhaps the teaching methodology itself was ineffective, making the learning process for the student nearly impossible. I have seen that happen at times. If it was the Apostle Paul who was doing the teaching,[4] the assumption of dull and ignorant could possibly be assumed. However, not all teachers conduct their lessons with clarity and under the unction of the Holy Spirit. The conscientious teacher will seek to effectively and convincingly teach their charge, with the goal of pleasing the Master. This begins with being:

Student Centered

When teaching, if the student is not learning, we dare not solely blame the student. It must be determined what possible weakness within the teacher or materials are limiting the effective communication of truth so a student cannot clearly understand it. The teacher is responsible for the communication, which should flow from the integrity of character in an instructor who is fully prepared, one who is:

Always Learning

An educator must be fascinated with the learning

---

[4] It is true that on one occasion Paul, preaching what some have termed an "everlasting Gospel" put a young man to sleep, causing him to fall out a window to his death. Some speculate that since many lamps and candles were lit, depleting the room of oxygen, s many likely fell asleep, to lesser consequences. (Acts 20:7-10) However, in spite of this, it is apparent that Paul, being raised in the Pharisaical tradition and under the anointing of the Holy Spirit, was a highly effective teacher of the Word of God.

process, for we never do obtain it all. The pursuit of knowledge should not be in vain, but focused on being constantly fresh, increasing our ability to impart new truth and revelation to openhearted students. Therefore, we teach out of a heart of love and compassion for the students. This is to be done with recognition that every student will learn at a slightly different rate. That is why the teacher must be patient, fully aware of the differing needs of individuals, and able to effectively teach each one in submission to the Holy Spirit and the Word of God.

CHAPTER THREE

PRINCIPLE 3: THE COMMISSION

When Jesus began His earthly ministry, He began as a *"teacher who has come from God,"* (John 3:1-2). This is not to minimize his role as Savior. He accomplished our salvation through His death on the cross and resurrection from the dead. But, His primary focus of ministry was to raise up leadership for the next generation. Thus, Jesus poured His life into His disciples, demonstrating for us a vital ministry principle, valid for today. In order to fulfill our purpose in ministry, we must learn to be effective in our teaching, having a similar focus in our teaching as did Christ. That purpose is to make disciples, preparing leadership for the outpouring of the Holy Spirit expected in every generation.

The first and primary reason for establishing the training of God's people in the local church is the commission given by Christ to His apostles. In Matthew 28:19, Jesus states:

"Therefore go and make disciples of all nations."

Matthew 28 speaks about the authority that was given to Jesus in heaven and earth, and was subsequently given to His disciples. Their commission was to go forth and make disciples of the nations. The process they were to follow included the preaching the Word of God, baptizing in the name of the Father, The Son and the Holy Spirit, then teaching the converted to do all that Jesus commanded, all by the grace of God. God is with the teacher in the classroom as he or she submits to the Lordship of Christ. If we are in a place of authority to teach students, then we need not struggle to gain authority, we must simply act based upon our God-given mandate.

This "Ministry Mandate" was given to the apostles, to teach the principles of Christ until men and women could live as Christ intended. This mandate encompassed much more than just making new converts; it called for the discipleship of nations. That is, the nations were to be given the opportunity to receive or deny Christ and His supremacy. If received, they would also be grafted into the family of God, the covenant of Abraham. If not, the judgment of the Lord would be measured out to them, though His grace and mercy would give ample opportunity for repentance.

The disciples received that commission, though unfortunately they were limited in their vision to Jerusalem. Salvation for the Jews was their heart, though the Father's heart cry included the Gentiles. Throughout history, this commission has been transferred from one generation to the next, and we are the recipients of that same wonderful mandate. Thus, today we must recognize the commission's call on our lives, to continue the proclamation of the

Gospel of Christ until the whole world is filled with the knowledge of the glory of the Lord *"as the waters cover the sea,"* (Habakkuk 2:14).

As we can learn from the Book of Acts (Acts 1:8, 2:1-5; 47), the only way we can see the Kingdom of God expand is through the planting of indigenous New Testament churches. The work of the apostle and prophet, working together, provides the foundation and vision for the local community. This dynamic method of expanding the kingdom can only occur as young men and women are properly trained and equipped to go to the nations, full of faith and the Holy Spirit, able to speak with boldness the unsearchable riches of Christ. The commission of Christ mandates to us all to properly train men and women for Christian service, for local church and the workplace, and the New Testament laboratory for such training is the local church.

CHAPTER FOUR

PRINCIPLE 4: THE CALL OF GOD

In a previous chapter we began to look at some of the basic biblical principles and scriptural references relating to teaching. Only a brief overview was presented; there are many other scriptures that could be applied to the teaching ministry. This chapter will review the primary aspects of an "ordained" teacher from the Old Testament perspective, to be followed by New Testament models.

The Teacher Was Called

The Old Testament presents several models of men who were primarily teachers. The first and most important is the parent. Deuteronomy 6:4 and beyond speaks about the vital responsibility of the parent, especially the father, as a role model for the teacher. In many families today, the role of teacher has been fully delegated to the mother. In our culture, it is often true that the mother has significantly more time for the teaching and training of the child. But, the father is still responsible for seeing to it that the teaching and training of children from a biblical perspective

31

is maintained within the home.

As God's progressive revelation was unveiled in the Old Testament, specialized leaders emerged who were able to effectively impart the truth of God's Word to His people. They included the scribe, the priest, and the prophet.

The Scribe

Scribes were writers or secretaries, primarily men, who copied the sacred scriptures and other important documents. The scribe was given the task of copying parchment pages in perfect detail. No mistakes were allowed, or the scribe would have to destroy the copy and start again ... from the beginning. Further, well trained scribes, since they were so intimately knowledgeable of Holy Writ, would be called upon to expound scriptural truth to others. The scribe fulfilled a highly critical role in Old Testament history.

The Priest

The priests were the religious and ceremonial leaders in Old Testament times they functioned in an intermediary role between the people and God, conducting sacrifices and bringing worship to the Lord They also provided instruction, especially during the times of feasts, fastings and festivals, which were part of the daily life experiences of the Jews. They were responsible for the application of scripture that had to be faithfully copied by the scribes, and the carrying forth of the "thus saith the Lord" of the prophet.

The Prophet

The prophets or seers were men and women called by God to hear and proclaim the will, purpose, and intention of God. The prophets, often working in traveling bands known as "the school of the prophets," focused on proclaiming the Word of righteousness and the impending judgments of God to the nations of Israel and Judah. Their intensity was highly problematic to any king who was living in sin, while their proclamations brought hope and assurance to the righteous servant of God.

Ezra

One of the best models of an Old Testament teacher who thoroughly prepared himself for the ministry of teaching is seen in the life of Ezra.[5] Ezra was a young man, raised in a time of captivity for the children of Israel. The great days of the kingdom of David and Solomon had long since passed and the children of Israel, due to their disobedience to the purpose of God, were held captive in the nation of Babylon. In the seventh chapter of the Book of Ezra we find a fascinating picture of Ezra's preparation. Chapter seven, verse six states that, *"He was a teacher well versed in the Law of Moses... for the hand of the LORD his God was on him."* With God's favor (grace, good hand) upon his life, Ezra set himself in a direction of great destiny.

Ezra, being a scribe, would have been required to pay close attention to detail. Historically, a scribe had to

---

[5] For more on the life of Ezra, see the book, *Keys to Successful Living,* by Dr. Stan E. DeKoven.

33

transcribe the Word in perfect order for it to be acceptable. Any mistake would necessitate the destruction of the scroll he was working on. Ezra would have learned to become a skilled craftsman, paying close attention to small details to ensure that his labor was not in vain. This is a characteristic of most good educators. They do not allow distractions that could prevent them from fulfilling their mission, to come between them and their teaching of children, young people or adults.

Set One's Heart

Referring to verse 10, Ezra had purposed in his heart to prepare himself for effective service. *"For Ezra had devoted himself to the study and observance of the Law of the LORD, and to teaching its decrees and laws in Israel."* Presented here are three primary purposes that Ezra set his heart towards.

First, he set his heart to study the law of the Lord!

The first and foremost responsibility of every believer is to develop a relationship with the Lord based upon a thorough understanding of God's Word. It is the responsibility of teachers to see to it that clarity and understanding are achieved. It is essential for a believer to fix or set their heart on a thorough knowledge and understanding of the things of God so as to properly transmit God's principles to others.

To Do

Secondly, Ezra was to practice doing what he was

learning from the Word of God. This practice was actually two fold. First, he was to do or obey the things that he was learning as he studied the law of God. Secondly, and equally as important, he was to practice his area of ministry until he perfected it. That's why we place such a strong emphasis on the local church. It is in the church, under loving, watchful pastoral care, that a person can practice areas and aspects of ministry until they are mature enough for leadership.

Third, Ezra had a vision for service that took him well beyond his circumstances, into the fulfillment of a destiny hidden in God. The vision to teach in Israel was birthed in his heart as he studied the Word and remembered the words of the Prophet Jeremiah. God had promised to one day return Israel from its cruel captivity and repossess the house of God. This vision and promise was fulfilled for Ezra in Nehemiah 8, as he stepped into the role he had long prepared for.

The Overriding Plan

The overriding plan of God for teaching is presented in Deuteronomy 6, where a picture of God's intention for education is revealed:

> Deuteronomy 6:1-9 says, *"These are the commands, decrees and laws the LORD your God directed me to teach you to observe in the land that you are crossing the Jordan to possess, so that you, your children, and their children after them may fear the LORD your God as long as you live by keeping all his decrees and commands that I give you, and so that*

you may enjoy long life. Hear, O Israel, and be careful to obey so that it may go well with you and that you may increase greatly in a land flowing with milk and honey, just as the LORD, the God of your fathers, promised you. Hear O Israel: The LORD our God, the LORD is one. Love the LORD your God with all your heart and with all your soul and with all your strength. These commandments that I give you today are to be upon your hearts. Impress them on your children. Talk about them when you sit at home and when you walk along the road, when you lie down and when you get up. Tie them as symbols on your hands and bind them on your foreheads. Write them on the doorframes of your houses and on your gates."

God commanded, through Moses, that the teaching ministry was to be a primary function within the family and all of society. To know Who God is, to love the Lord God with all of one's ability and know how to live life to its fullest, based upon God's precepts, is the highest good. That is still the goal for modern times in church life. Part of the purpose for communicating God's truth is to create an understanding in His disciples as to what His purpose is for them, a purpose divinely determined from the beginning of time.

CHAPTER FIVE

PRINCIPLE 5: THE CHURCH

THE PLACE OF TRAINING

In our modern era, the local community church building is often the most underutilized space in the community. It is perfectly designed architecturally for multiple activities, including the teaching of theological subjects. Of course, the luxury of the type of facilities we enjoy today did not exist in Jesus' day. However, similar structures to local churches were used in the New Testament era for the training of believers.

In the New Testament, the most comprehensive picture of God's plan for training was modeled through the life of Christ. In John 3, Nicodemus made a very profound statement when he said,

> *"He came to Jesus at night and said, 'Rabbi, we know you are a teacher who has come from God. For no one could perform the miraculous signs you are doing if God were not with him"*

The primary focus of Christ's ministry was that of discipleship, or the transference of the Father's plan and purpose from His life into His disciples' lives. When they were finished with their educational program, the three and a half years they spent with Jesus here on earth, God's vision was for them to take up the mantle and carry on the traditions established by Christ. With this mantle they would be able to fully communicate everything that they had been taught and do everything that Jesus had done in the same way and the same measure that Jesus Himself did.

That should be the philosophical focus of every Christian leader. The education transmitted to a child or adult should produce life experiences with practical applications. When a child or adult has completed a class or program of training, they should be able to both communicate what they have learned and practice it in their daily lives. Thus, they become able to effectively develop their own potential to train others in the Lord.

Not only was teaching the focus of Jesus' ministry, but it became that of Paul the Apostle as well. In the Book of Acts, Paul joins Barnabas the Apostle, sitting at Barnabas' feet as an assistant instructor (Acts 11). His tutelage under Barnabas continued for a full year, where they jointly taught the disciples in the principles of Christ. It was in Antioch that believers in Jesus Christ were first called Christians (little Christs). They must have had a fairly effective teaching program for such a visible change of identity and character to occur. A good assumption is that Paul and Barnabas taught everything that Barnabas had learned while he sat at the feet of the apostles in Jerusalem, prior to his being sent to spy out Antioch (Acts 11).

Later the Apostle Paul continued in the same tradition. In the city of Ephesus (Acts 19), he focused his ministry, on the disciples who followed him, and for two years he taught them. They rented a facility called the School of Tyrannus and there he daily instructed the disciples.

What did he teach? Everything Barnabas and he had taught in Antioch, which was a continuation of everything that the apostles taught in Jerusalem. This in turn, was essentially everything that Jesus had taught and modeled to them. This dynamic process, of one generation teaching the next generation the plans and purposes of God must continue in our churches today if we are going to see Christ's purposes fulfilled in the 21st century.

The New Covenant Goal[6]

In 1 Timothy 1:5 we read,
> *"The goal of this command is love, which comes from a pure heart and a good conscience and a sincere faith."*

Paul's goal in teaching Timothy was to transform his life, changing his priorities. Timothy was one of the primary disciples of Paul, nurtured through Paul's teaching ministry. In this verse, the goal of his instruction is presented. Paul's goal became the goal of Timothy's teaching ministry at Ephesus as well. The first and most important goal was love, which flowed from a pure heart. Secondly, a good conscience or developing the mind of Christ was essential, and third, a sincere faith, or a faith that was to be openly proclaimed by committed saints was to be

---

[6] For more on the Goal of Teaching, see *Transferring the Vision* by Dr. DeKoven.

the result of spiritual instruction.

Pure Heart

Paul's focus of instruction was not just to stimulate the intellect or to provide facts and figures, but to ensure a process of purification in the disciples' heart. The love of God was to be seen and expressed in the life of the believer. True love is to flow from a purified heart, one that has been changed by an encounter with the Spirit of God through the Word of God.

Good Conscience

"A good conscience" indicates that through the process of teaching and the study of God's Word, a change should begin to occur in the thought life of the student/believer. This change occurs as they look into the mirror of truth found in God's Word. As they compare their life to the Word of God, areas of deficiency in need of correction are revealed. As confession of sin or failure is accomplished and repentance is completed, the process of change takes effect. Ultimately, this process creates a clean and clear conscience, free from all guilt and anxiety related to these past mistakes or sins. Further, it changes our perception of life from self to being God focused.

Sincere Faith

Finally, a sincere faith is essential. This means faithfulness to the task that God has called us to. Whatever training a student is involved in, the expectation is that when they have completed it, they will be faithful to perform what they have been trained to do. It is not enough to learn something without making a practical application.[7] Jesus taught with an eternal focus in mind. What the disciples saw Christ do, they did. Paul worked from the same central concept. It is vitally important for teachers as leaders to emphasize theory, theology and effective practice, faithful to perform according to the knowledge and skills acquired over time.

The Biblical Perspective

As emphasized earlier, all instruction should be accomplished either within the home or through the auspices of the local church. This does not mean that other institutions are not serving the Lord and the primary focus of control of the educational process. The teacher must be able to teach to the best of their ability as commissioned by the Lord, according to the grace that God has given them and the measure of faith provided. Whether one is an active five-fold ministry member or has the gift, ability, and desire to teach, all need to do so to the best of their ability as commissioned by the Master Teacher Himself.

To Grow Up

Referring back to Ephesians 4:11-12, the concern or goal of instruction is to bring students to maturity. The focus of the teaching ministry of the apostle was precisely that. It was certainly the focus of Christ. If the focus was perfection, then both Jesus and Paul failed miserably. None of their students were paragons of perfection. Their goal and ours is not perfection, but maturity. Maturity can be

---

[7] More on this in the conclusion.

seen in the ability to rightly divide or understand God's truth and transmit it in spite of human frailties. Having the same concerns that God has for the students will assist us to remain on track despite our failures. The goals of instruction go far beyond teaching the brightest to shine (which they no doubt will do with us or without us), or attaining the highest grade point averages, but to ensure that the character of Christ is formed in the hearts of His people.

The Craft of Teaching[8]

When speaking about the teachers' craft, we are referring to the tools of the trade. In order to have an effective teaching center, the tools of the trade must be readily available, and we must know how to wield them.

II Timothy 2:15, NAS speaks of a prime purpose of the teaching of the Word of God.

"Study to show thyself approved unto God, a workman that needeth not to be ashamed, rightly dividing the word of truth."

An instructor's study must be diligent, with a focus. That focus is to understand the Word and communicate it with clarity and conviction. This brings the reader to the next point, which is the Word itself:

II Timothy 3:14-17 says, *"You, however, continue in the things you have learned and become convinced of, knowing from whom you have learned them, and*

---

[8] An expanded view of this is seen in "Transferring the Vision."

*that from childhood you have known the sacred
writings which are able to give you the wisdom that
leads to salvation through faith which is in Christ
Jesus. All scripture is inspired by God and profitable
for teaching, for reproof, for correction, for training
and righteousness; so that the man of God may be
adequate, equipped for every good work."*

The word "adequate" used here simply means "to be
equipped or fully trained," able to apply the craft of
teaching within an organized structure. The Word of God is
able to change the hearts and minds of men and women.

That is why we teach God's Word. Our focus is to first
learn and then transmit what is learned with accuracy, so
that others may comprehend the fullness of meaning.

Teaching and Vision

Habakkuk 2:1-3, KJV states, *"I will stand upon
my watch, and set me upon the tower, and will watch
to see what he will say unto me, and what I shall
answer when I am reproved. And the LORD answered
me, and said, 'Write the vision, and make it plain upon
tables, that he may run that reads it. For the vision is
yet for an appointed time, but at the end it shall speak,
and not lie: though it tarry, wait for it; because it will
surely come, it will not tarry."*

Teaching must flow from a vision; a vision which is a
part of the heart of God. The vision includes the ability to
see students differently than they were when they first
began their journey in Christ. Teachers must have a vision

43

for their students that will take them far beyond their present level of knowledge to where God wants them to be. In order to do so, we who are called to teach must receive a vision from the Lord for the students' transformation through the revelation of the truth of the Word, by the inspired instruction presented. Much prayer should be a part of the process. It helps to set aside quality time with the Lord, being willing to accept correction if the vision for the students is less than God's perspective. God can and will provide clear vision of the potential for each student being instructed.

Further, the Word says to *"write the vision, make it plain,"* or make it clear, so that those who read it will *"run with it,"* or proclaim it! The instructor's goal is to communicate their subject matter with sufficient clarity and inspiration for the student to proclaim that same instruction to others. The hope is to take the most problematic students, those who present the greatest challenges, and impart to them a sense of hope and belief in themselves and their God. With this confidence the student will do more than they ever thought possible. Part of our craft is to encourage the learner to learn, motivating the student to study and learn through vision is a major key to the teaching and learning process.

It is helpful in a teaching ministry to write down the vision God gives for a student who is being taught. This personal touch takes time, but it is well worth the effort, as through the eyes of faith students will outstretch and exceed the expectations of both student and teacher. The vision must be positive, looking for the good and extracting from the students their very best through the teaching process. With positive effort, and by the grace of God, the student will grow in knowledge, understanding, and wisdom. If we are professional in our approach, diligent in our application of proven teaching methodology, and if our character and hearts are right before God with a focus to assist the student, positive results will be evident.

Systematic Instruction

In Acts 11 and later in Acts 19, Paul and Barnabas taught the disciples in a systematic and organized fashion. Their program of instruction was neither haphazard nor slipshod. Some might view the teaching ministry of Jesus as "Laissez-faire," or the "teach as we go" type of instructional format. Nothing that Jesus did was by accident, however. His ministry was personally orchestrated by the Father!

Jesus, in perfect obedience to the voice of His Father, taught His disciples until they internalized the Teacher as a living model. This internalized or impartational model prepared them to effectively train others in the future. They were organized and systematic, beginning with foundational teachings and principles, building on them, line upon line, precept upon precept.

Since all students begin at a slightly different baseline, understanding the relative strengths and weaknesses of the student is very important. It is the teacher's responsibility to organize the instruction and teach the material in a systematic fashion. The expectation is to provide for each student the opportunity to learn at his or her highest possible level of achievement, moving forward from one foundation to another.

The Pauline Model

Paul the Apostle was a highly disciplined instructor. In his writings, Paul painstakingly transitions from one principle to the next. Building slowly, precept upon precept, the reader is able to follow the progression of his thoughts (though the Apostle Peter had difficulty with some of his letters). Teachers need to instruct with purpose and fluidity, as did Paul. To be fluid, one must be organized and prepared.

A part of the teacher's craft is to see the anointing and authority that God gives, inherent in the role as teacher, released on behalf of the student. Along with the authority that God gives, the Lord will also provide "unction," or an anointing from the Holy Spirit. God's Word will never return void or empty. Thus, when teaching the Word of God, know that there is an anointing, an unction that is already on God's Word which is able to penetrate the heart and mind of the most difficult student. God has given great authority to those called to teach His Word, and gives an equal anointing to teach and communicate truth, so that it will effectively change hearts and minds, preparing God's people for activation in service according to their unique gifts and calling.

CHAPTER SIX

PRINCIPLE 6: THE COMPANY

AN APOSTOLIC TEAM

DELIVERING A COMPREHENSIVE PROGRAM

The New Testament goal of teaching was to establish maturity in men and women and to create Apostolic Companies for future ministry expansion and church planting. When Paul or Peter ministered in a new city, their goal was to establish a teaching center and then a church (Acts 11, 13, 19). However, they did not go alone. They always took with them a team of trained leaders from a given city to assist in various aspects of ministry. Thus, when a church was planted it was done by a team under apostolic and prophetic authority, built on a strong and sure foundation. They did not work with novices, but took adults fully trained in the local church for the expansion of the Kingdom of God.

In the 21st century, we must regain the perspective of the New Testament, and return to the philosophy of training found in the pages of God's Word. This can only be done through education and training in the local church.

47

About Teaching Adults

Adult education includes both the highly practical as well as theological areas of instruction.

Briefly, Adult Christian Education should be comprised of two fundamental and foundational components. They are the practical education and training of families in daily living, from birth to the grave, and Theological or Biblical education.

A family ministry curriculum will provide courses in adult education that are practical and relevant to the needs of the community. Such courses as Marriage and Family Life, Communication Skills, Single Parenting, Financial Planning, as well as Divorce and Remarriage courses are needed. These courses can be offered, usually at very little cost, and are often presented by Christian experts within the local community. Training courses can significantly enhance the overall growth and development of the adults within a caring Christian community, as well as provide evangelistic opportunities within the community at large.

Christian parenting is one of the biggest needs in society today, especially in light of society's numerous ills. The increase in domestic violence and child abuse is abhorrent, even in Christian circles, and can be eradicated to a great extent by education and support systems that the church of the locality[9] can provide. Unfortunately, the church has, by and large, neglected confronting these issues

---

[9] When I refer to the church of the locality, I am specifically addressing the possible unified consortium that can and should be developed in local communities, where churches of all types band together for a greater purpose, whether for missions, education, or evangelistic outreach.

from a biblical perspective. Practical curriculum as a part of the adult education program designed to address the growing needs of a secularized culture are essential.

Another part of a practical curriculum should include the standard adult Sunday school level courses in Biblical Studies, such as the study of certain books of the Bible or various topics and themes within the Word of God that every believer needs to understand. This should include foundational courses such as a "New Believer's Class," courses in "Old Testament" and "New Testament," as well as courses discussing issues of importance such as the "Fruit of the Spirit," the "Gifts of the Holy Spirit," etc.

Along with practical studies, and in light of the churches' responsibility to train present and future leaders, there is a demonstrated need for leadership training. Adults are hungry to be trained in Biblical Studies and Theology, along with advanced ministry skills.

Adult education can be extremely effective, and provided at low cost. Many new paradigm institutions within the United States have developed such alternative services. From video-based programs to complete Bible College and Theological training courses, advanced education for ministry and leadership can be made available to a local church as a part of or an extension of an existing College or Bible Institute. These systems can be implemented in a cost-effective way, becoming a tremendous blessing for the local community. Further, multi-cultural programs are readily available in numerous formats. Generally, local faculty can train leadership for a church or a group of churches, developing men and women in their specific areas of gifting. Many of these students will become church workers, church planters, or members of church staffs as full-time ministers.

Young Adults

One group needing specialized attention is the young adult. Educational processes are to continue throughout life. The young adult stage of development, coinciding with ages 18-24, is called the *mountain top* age. Physical maturity has been reached (for most), and the major decisions of marriage, vocational choices, etc. are all being negotiated. The young adult is becoming much more mature and rounded in their personality, even though they still struggle with important life issues.

Young adults often resist and rebel against strong dogmatic or highly religious rules and regulations. Because of their intellectual capabilities and deep desire for intimacy along with closeness and meaning in relationships, curriculum developed for this age group must focus on relational wholeness. The young man or woman's relationship to church, God, the opposite sex, work, etc., should be addressed with frankness and openness. Further, vocational choices, being so very critical to success in life, are often topics for instruction and dialog.

Further, strong convictions are being formed, hopefully in a positive vein toward Christ and the church. Thus, young adulthood can be one of the periods where the greatest potential service for Christ can occur. Sincere life commitments in this age group can often lead to fulltime Christian ministry. Even if full-time ministry is not the goal, encouragement to serve the Lord in the workplace should always be emphasized. If service of the Lord does not begin at this age, it seldom will in later life. To live is to serve, and young adults, with their abundance of energy and enthusiasm have an ability to give and receive help for life's challenges. Thus, a strong emphasis on teaching the Bible with practical life application is of greatest benefit.

This brief description of the educational needs of adults lays a foundation for understanding those needs and the special concerns they present to the church. Church leaders must recognize that each adult has differing needs that must be addressed in creating an effective ministry within the local church.

God has given a mandate to leaders in the Body of Christ to train and educate God's precious people from birth to grave (Ephesians 4:11-17). That learning process never ends. All education and training programs are designed to prepare God's people for future life with Him. Thus, educational efforts that include training within the church of the locality must be pursued, from a kingdom perspective, with eternal perspective.

CHAPTER SEVEN

PRINCIPLE 7: THE CURRICULUM

THE MODERN CHURCH

There are a number of different ways to develop adult education programs. In liturgically oriented churches, there are usually well developed catechism instruction which begins early in a young person's life and continues through adulthood.

Adults primarily receive their education in a Sunday school class or perhaps in a home fellowship. Unfortunately, there has not been sufficient emphasis on teaching that leads to clear biblical understanding. In fact, some have said that the church in America is biblically illiterate. The need for more effective programs for local church training is evident.

One cannot rely on Sunday morning or Sunday evening services alone to instruct people towards maturity. All adults should be fully trained and equipped to do their part in the Kingdom of God, and this requires time.

This is especially true in light of God's mandate to

bring His people to maturity, to fully disciple whole nations or ethnic groups. To do this, systematic training programs across the entire spectrum of church endeavors are needed. In response to this acute need, many churches have established complete Bible College programs or Training Institutes within their local assembly.

There are many excellent ministries that can assist local churches to develop a comprehensive adult education program. Many are highly effective in releasing people into the areas of their unique gifting and calling. What should the components of a good adult education program include?

A Place

As stated earlier, the local church facility is the most underutilized building in most communities. However, a limited venue need not limit your ability to train. We have seen Bible training in houses, rented facilities, local churches, and even in the open air. However, the local church is by far the most ideal... and usually available venue for training.

People

For many local churches, this is no problem. The people are readily available and hungry for the Word. However, a survey of the community may be wise to determine how solid the interest in a Bible College program really is. There is nothing worse than starting a program and seeing it close due to lack of interest. We must weigh the cost before launching any ministry.

Assuming our goal is to transform an individual, new

convert into a dynamic disciple for Christ, we must ask ourselves "What courses are needed to accomplish the task?"

A Systematic Curriculum

First of all, success requires that there be a series of courses offered in basic doctrine. The foundational doctrines of the faith would include: baptism, salvation, Who God is, Who Christ is, Who the Holy Spirit is, etc. These are needed to establish a strong foundation of faith. There should also be general courses providing the knowledge of the purposes and use of the gifts of the Holy Spirit. Courses must also be offered detailing what a Christian family is like, answering practical questions like, "How do I handle my finances?" These are basic teachings that must be included in each course provided for new converts.

Secondly, a solid curriculum will offer courses of instruction in the building of godly character. An emphasis of instruction within the teaching program is to conform one's will to the will of God as found within the Word of God. The only way to do this is to challenge adult believers to look into the mirror of truth found within the scriptures with a willingness to change through the process of repentance, or a change of thinking. Changed thinking leads to a change of lifestyle! Solomon said it like this, *"For as he* (a man) *thinks in his heart, so is he"* (Proverbs 23:7, NAS). And Paul added,

"And be not conformed to this world: but be ye transformed by the renewing of your mind, that ye may

prove what is that good, and acceptable, and perfect, will of God," (Romans 12:2, NAS).

Thus, one must be confronted with issues of sin or wrong belief through teaching. The best time to do this is when a new convert is young in the Lord. In fact, it is best not to wait until they have learned religious defenses to protect them from the "onslaught of God's Word." In reality, there are many hardened saints of God who remain entrenched in sinful and destructive life patterns because they have been hurt through past relationships. They consequently have become unwilling to open their hearts to the Word of God. When a new convert enters the church, they are naturally open and teachable. It is fairly easy to work with them individually or in a small group, thus making a powerful impact on their lives. It is in the beginning of their walk in God that the learning of fundamentals is vital, and it is possible to work through the problem areas of life, coming to maturity and wholeness in God.

Third, adults need to be taught practical ministry. That is, they need to have courses on how the gifts of the Holy Spirit work, how to study the Word of God effectively, and studies about the dynamics of the Christian life. Further, courses should be offered which effectively present doctrinal and theological topics, and answer the difficult questions that adults grapple with. After all, what do the various commonly used church words mean, like salvation, justification, sanctification, propitiation, etc.? Other topics may include, "How is one supposed to treat their neighbors? What is evangelism and how does one learn to evangelize?"

These topics and many more, are germane for the adult learner. Each course should provide a textbook, study guide, exam (for those seeking college credit), teaching notes for the instructor, and so on. Of course, each church needs a coordinator for the adult ministry, which is made easy if the church is linked with an existing educational network.

These systematic courses, offered within local church structure, are readily available and extremely powerful. An adult education program helps the equipping of the saints and releasing men and women into fully serving God within their local church and beyond. Also, as the Holy Spirit moves on people's lives, we will release them into greater areas of service. Often, evangelists, teachers, pastors, prophets and apostles are raised up within the local church and released from that community of faith to expand God's Kingdom. Those sent would always keep a tie to the home church, a New Testament pattern seen in the book of Acts through the ministry of the Paul the apostle.

A Delivery System

Before launching such a program, a determination must be made as to how the program is to be taught. There are many options. They include live classroom instruction, seminars, audio, video, mentorship, correspondence, Internet, full or part-time course offerings, and so on. A leadership team at a Local Church must carefully choose the right methodology for working in their community. Thus, if working with an existing resource ministry, such as an educational network, flexibility in the delivery system is vital. A flexible and well-thought-out program along with cost considerations are the two biggest factors contributing to the lack of success in programs for local churches.

Teachers

The selection of teachers for a program is equally or more important than the setting or curriculum. An anointed and well prepared teacher is essential to the success of a program. Most local churches have highly qualified individuals already in place who can teach. Many of the network schools can provide faculty either live or via video/DVD, or local instructors can be found in other local churches, which opens the door to effective networking church to church, which is a vital step toward unity for a city. In any case, the local Apostle/Pastor of the program must have the final authority to determine who will teach his or her people in the local setting.

Adult Education

Adult education is vital, as are all areas of education within the church. One cannot emphasize enough the importance of it. It was important in the life of Moses. He (through his scribe) wrote down all the things that had occurred from creation until the time he went home to be with the Lord. Throughout the Old Testament, scribes wrote down important events even as they were inspired by the Holy Spirit. These are known to us today as the Old Testament Scriptures. In the New Testament, the pattern of the life of Christ, seen in His teaching of children, where He blessed them, nurturing them all the way through adulthood, is evident. He ministered both practically and profoundly to bring about the purposes of God.

In the life of Peter and Paul, as with all the apostles, the same basic program of teaching and training, equipping people for further service is seen. Throughout church history one can observe the importance of teaching to impart the truth of who Jesus Christ is, to the *"whosoever wills"* that come into the house of the Lord.

God is building His Kingdom. He builds His Kingdom foundationally, line upon line, precept upon precept. He wants to build it strong, with a firm and solid apostolic and prophetic foundation. That foundation can be positively and powerfully laid through a teaching ministry that is systematic and comprehensive.

It should be found in and through the local church... yours!

CONCLUSION

PREPARATION FOR ACTIVATION

Of course, the reason for equipping/educating God's people is to activate them. By activation I mean to see every believer emerge, through the teaching/impartation of God's word, with gifts to be used (see 1 Corinthians 12:14-18, Ephesians 4:11-16, Romans 6-13) according to the measure of faith (Romans 12:3) God has given.

Not all believers are called to church leadership, but all can serve, whether in the local church or the church in the workplace. It should be the goal of every spiritual leader to see the 80% of inactive Christians (according to Barna's latest statistics) activated into service.

A greater goal is to see the Kingdom of God expanded through church planting. Establishing New Testament churches everywhere is the key to revival. It is my hope that every local church congregation, cooperating with other congregations in the locality, work to see every believer trained, activated, and released into God's harvest field.

APPENDIX I

DEFINITIONS

1. The Church, ecclesia, means the "ones called out," gathered together, with capability to govern in locality (see Acts) and is made up of all born again believers throughout the ages. In the New Testament pattern there were numerous local expressions of the church, which was referred to as a church in a particular locality, commonly a city (such as the church in Antioch, Jerusalem, Ephesus, etc.). The church universal, made up of all believers from all ages, has always been expressed in some sort of local gathering under divine order and appropriate leadership.

2. Churches; always discussed in context of a greater region than a city such as the churches in Asia; modern equivalent would be churches in a major metropolis or county such as Los Angeles County.

3. Congregations; the gathering of believers under local elder(s) within a city. These collective congregations together make up the church within a particular city locality.

APPENDIX II

RECOMMENDED READING

BY DR. STAN DEKOVEN

"Keys to Successful Living," Vision Publishing.
"Catch the Vision: How to Get a Vision for Your Life and Ministry," Vision Publishing.
"Visionary Leadership," Vision Publishing.
"Pastoral Ministry: In The Eye of the Storm," Vision Publishing.
"Supernatural Architecture: Preparing the Church for the 21st Century," Wagner Publishing.

BY DR. C. PETER WAGNER

"Your Spiritual Gifts Can Help Your Church Grow," Regal Books, 1994.
"How To Have a Healing Ministry In Any Church," Regal Books, 1988.
"Prayer Shield," Regal Books, 1992.
"Praying With Power" Regal Books, 1997.
"Church quake!," Regal Books, 1999.

BY DR. KEN CHANT

"Better Than Revival," Vision Publishing
"Building the Church God Wants" Vision Publishing
"Christian Life," Vision Publishing
"Pentecostal Pulpit," Vision Publishing
"Understanding Your Bible," Vision Publishing
"The Church," by Barry Chant, Vision Publishing (Dr.
    Ken Chant, General Editor)

BY DR. DAVID SHIBLEY

"Once in a Lifetime." Sovereign World ltd.
*"What Christians Should Know About... The End Time
    Harvest."* Sovereign World ltd.
"A Force in The Earth." Creation House

By Dr. Tim Dailey

" Bringing Heaven to Earth," Vision Publishing

ABOUT THE AUTHOR

Dr. Stan DeKoven is a licensed Marriage, Family and Child Counselor in California, working for many years in the field. He is the Founder and President of the Vision International Education Network, with programs including Vision International University and the Vision International Extension Institute Network of Resource Centers worldwide, Vision Publishing, The American Society of Christian Therapists and the Family Care Network. He is the author of over 30 books in practical Christian living for the maturing of God's people. Dr. DeKoven was married to his beautiful wife Karen, until her passing in January 2000, has two daughters, Rebecca and Rachel, and three grandchildren.

For more information on the Vision International Education Network or to receive catalogs on the books and seminars of Dr. Stan DeKoven and other Vision writers and teachers, write or call:

VISION INTERNATIONAL
1115 D STREET
RAMONA, CA 92065
1-800-9-VISION
WWW.VISION.EDU
WWW.VISIONPUBLISHINGSERVICES.COM